CW00825788

Kristen Lindquist

island

copyright © 2023 Kristen Lindquist

ISBN 978-1-958408-28-5

Red Moon Press
PO Box 2461
Winchester VA
22604-1661 USA
www.redmoonpress.com

Cover: "Alice Brown". Courtesy of the
Monhegan Museum of Art & History.

first printing

In memory of my grandparents

Ruth & Wally Lindquist

*who inspired my love of islands
by taking me as a child to Lime Island,
Monhegan, Isle of Skye, and Orkney*

"What seas what shores what grey rocks
   and what islands
What water lapping the bow
And scent of pine and the woodthrush
   singing through the fog
What images return
O my daughter."

— *from* "Marina" *by* T.S. Eliot (1931)

island

sunlight and fog

Offerings

An island ten miles off the coast of Maine,
a pocket beach, one early spring morning.
Past a granite seawall that blooms with sun-
burst lichen, I poke through detritus left by
the low tide: sea-worn pebbles and beach
glass, mussel shells, discarded lobster claws
and the rubber bands that held them closed,
disintegrating bait bags, fragments of chim-
ney brick, pottery shards, lemon rinds, fish
bones . . .

    waving offshore
    beyond the rusted shipwreck
    kelp strands

I tuck into my pocket every yellow peri-
winkle I find until I have a whole handful
of yellow, unlike any other color on this
beach — a hopeful, solar yellow with a little
seawater trapped inside like a microscopic
sloshing tide. To what small ear can I hold
up this shell? What distant ocean will sing
from its spiraling core?

onshore breeze
the herring weathervane
turns into it

Each tiny shell's an empty house, absent
now of whatever consciousness a snail pos-
sesses. A jangling heap of shells rattling in
my pocket, tiny exoskeletons of calcium
carbonate. I shake them out onto the sand
as if their pattern could reveal some kind of
augury. If only I knew what to ask.

his song amplified
by morning fog
yellow warbler

a Morse code S
tapped into the maple . . .
first sapsucker

worm moon
the owl's small body
still warm

neap tide
a warbler chases sand fleas
along the wrack line

winter blowdowns
the dense tangle
of wren song

sunlight and fog
mingle with spruces
a kinglet's thin song

slack tide
beach stones exposed
where they are

desire lines —
a long vee of cormorants
streams past the moon

working harbor
the tide's slow progress
up the wharf ladder

some stories
take all day to tell
red-eyed vireo

ebbing tide . . .
I text him a photo
of a heart-shaped rock

spruce-filtered light
a raven tells the island
I'm here

grey seals in surf
the tingling skin
of my selkie self

loose strands of rockweed . . .
a small boy splashes
into his father's arms

ready or not . . .
a girl aligns her body
with an apple tree

the smoothest beach stone
seals waiting offshore
for low tide

new moon
a harpooned tuna
hangs from the stern

first day of fall
the dead snake's tail
still twitching

storm surge
heavy metal blares
from the fish house

first frost
orioles raid
the grape arbor

autumn gale
a crowd of propane tanks
huddles on the wharf

frost on marsh grass
a harrier glides past
the no-hunting sign

snow falling offshore . . .
a gull swallows
another star

an arrowhead
almost a rock again
winter storm watch

north wind
porcupine tooth marks
scar a sapling

flotsam

Washed Up

Alone, lying half-asleep on the beach in the fog, sleeve over my face, feeling a little sorry for myself, it's easy to imagine the osprey's cry an alarm to wake me or to express some avian concern over my inert form. But really, the bird doesn't even know I'm here, my body just another piece of flotsam tossed among the shells and seaweed.

more than one way
to look at it
beach glass

a lone crow
wipes its bill on a branch
mud season

deer trail . . .
the wood frogs fall silent
at my approach

island birthday
he tosses another shell
onto the midden

puffs of pollen
a warbler's passage
through the spruce

the old dory
planted with tulips
making do

fogbow
the catbird's song
mostly water

climbing the cliff trail
the exhaust
of a lobster boat

cormorants airing out
the dark underbellies
of rainclouds

all the eiders
dive at once
the pulse of surf

wild strawberries
picking my way
along the shore trail

a quartz vein
running up the cliff face
— first gull chicks

neon buoys . . .
a pod of porpoises
crosses our wake

fairy house trail
pretending
I've lost my way

spruce forest
finding refuge
from other hikers

old quarry . . .
a buck in the underbrush
holds my stare

hay-scented ferns
a host of white moths
rises as we pass

off-season trap-yard
piles of coiled rope entangled
with knotweed

the way out . . .
amanita mushrooms
on both sides of the trail

young gulls
scrounging windfall apples
island schoolyard

harbor moonrise
a voice in the dark
whispers *whoa*

king tide
the last bit of beach
pocked with deer tracks

a long marriage . . .
storm-heaped seaweed
hides the path

must everything die
question marks alight
on fallen apples

this slow forgetting . . .
a gull's feather flags
the wrack line

lighthouse

Island

Life can be this simple: a room with a green floor and white walls, tacked up image of the Last Supper, cracked ceramic ewer in a bowl on a small white table by the window. An oil lamp to draw moths to the screens. A neat outhouse, a well with sweet water. Enough food for your stay. A small pebble beach at the end of a narrow, steep trail. Osprey overhead. And the visual indulgence of phlox, daylilies, daisies, rugosa blooming along a stoic, lichen-spattered stone wall. All you need, and yet . . .

signs of deer we never see understory

what woke me —
silhouettes of spruces point
to Polaris

island sunrise
a light already on
in someone's kitchen

beach peas in bloom
a bunting whistles up
the sun

lifting fog
the loud clear song
of the fox sparrow

island garden
tangled heaps of seaweed
mark the fallow rows

rain drips from new leaves . . .
the indigo bunting's
last brown feather

free-range chickens
peck around a junked truck
independence day

one morning in Maine
wet webs
tent the yard

bushwhacking
a pheasant's squawk
unexpectedly close

fishermen's graveyard
a view of the sea
from every stone

rising tide
a young girl wades in
up to her belly button

morning fog
my closest neighbors
are tiger lilies

gathering clouds
the click of mah-jongg tiles
on a card table

no hint
of what's to come
blackberries in bloom

bleak sky
a soaring gull catches
no light

Monhegan cliffs
between here and Europe
one fishing boat

noon ferry
halfway across the bay
a monarch keeps pace

calm before the storm
the voices of fishermen
carry to shore

island sunset
someone rows a red dory
out of the harbor

sunset glow . . .
a line of waxwings
fills a bare branch

autumn twilight
the lighthouse beacon turns on
the dark

all the ripe peaches
stolen from the tree
spill of moonlight

harvest moon
the lights of tuna boats
wait offshore

shells at low tide
finding the constellation
that points to home

salt spray
this body
of water

Salt Air

A friend of mine keeps a herd of goats on a small island off a slightly larger island way off the coast of Maine. From across the harbor you can often see the goats picking their way, one after another, along trails they've worn in the thin soil. Other times, they're out of sight for days, their bleats carried by fog.

following seas
the toll of a bell buoy
grows louder

My friend was off-island for several days and returned to utter chaos: the goats had broken into her house and trashed it. The animals ate all the grain, as well as anything else they could find that was remotely edible, and despoiled every surface, including her bed. Days later when I ask how the clean-up is going, she says that even with all the

windows open, everything in the house still
smells like goat.

    each lobster boat
    trailed by a cloud of gulls
    mouths to feed

Acknowledgments

Thank you to the editors of the following publications in which some of these poems, or earlier versions of these poems, first appeared:

Acorn – "beach peas in bloom" (50)

Akitsu Quarterly – "island birthday" (Spring/ Summer 2023), "puffs of pollen" (Fall 2019), "off-season trap-yard" (Fall 2022), "harvest moon" (Winter 2021), "shells at low tide" (Spring 2020)

Blithe Spirit – "a lone crow" (32.3), "hay-scented ferns" (31.2), "gathering clouds" (32.1), "sunset glow" (32.4)

bottle rockets – "morning fog" (45)

Cattails – "the way out" (April 2022)

Cold Moon Journal – "north wind" (2.7.21), "lifting fog" (4.6.22)

Contemporary Haibun 17 (Rich Youmans, editor; Red Moon Press, 2022) – "Washed Up"

Contemporary Haibun Online – "Salt Air" (17.3)

Drifting Sands Haibun – "harbor moonrise" (21; in haibun "The Point Being"), "Island" (10)

#FemkuMag – "Washed Up" (31), "rising tide" (27)

First Frost – "an arrowhead" (5), "what woke me" (3)

Frogpond – " free-range chickens" (45.2)

The Haiku Calendar 2023 (Snapshot Press, 2022) – "north wind"

The Haiku Foundation's Haiku Dialogue – "winter blowdowns" (6.17.21)

hedgerow – "the smoothest beach stone" (141), "deer trail" (142), "all the ripe peaches" (141)

The Heron's Nest – "cormorants airing out" (24.3)

The Island Reader – "Offerings" (2020)

Kingfisher – "ready or not" (6), "a quartz vein" (6)

Mann Library's Daily Haiku – "puffs of pollen," "wild strawberries" (Oct. 2020)

Modern Haiku – "loose strands of rockweed" (53.1), "new moon" (52.3), "island sunrise" (52.1)

New England Letters – "spruce-filtered light" (97), "first frost" (113), "frost on marsh grass" (121), "young gulls" (89)

Poetry Pea Podcast – "grey seals in surf," "the old dory," "island sunrise," "fishermen's graveyard" (Season 4, Episode 9)

Presence – "a Morse code S" (74), "neap tide" (67), "working harbor" (69), "all the eiders" (70), "spruce forest" (76), "island garden" (72), "island sunset" (73)

Tandem: the Rengay Journal – "must everything die" (1.1; in rengay "Symmetry" with Alan S. Bridges)

tinywords – "some stories" (22.1)

Trash Panda – "autumn gale" (4)

tsuri-dōrō – "ebbing tide" (14), "fairy house trail" (12), "rain drips from new leaves" (10)

The View Arcade: Two Autumns Anthology 2022 (Nathanael Tico, editor; Two Autumns Press, 2022) – "working harbor," "frost on marsh grass," "north wind," "island garden," "autumn twilight"

Wales Haiku Journal – "worm moon" (Autumn 2021), "slack tide" (Winter 2021-22)

What Weathers, What Returns: Anthology of the Broadmoor Haiku Collective (Red Moon Press, 2023) – "worm moon," "island sunset"

I also wish to express my gratitude to the Broadmoor Haiku Collective, with whom I found my home in haiku — with special thanks to Brad Bennett and Paul Miller for helping me shape this book — and to the Maine islands that inspired these poems: Bear, Brimstone, Clark, Deer Isle, Great Spruce Head, Hurricane, Mount Desert, North Haven, Vinalhaven, and, especially, Monhegan.

About the Author

KRISTEN LINDQUIST received her MFA in poetry from the University of Oregon. She has published several collections of non-haiku poetry and wrote a prize-winning nature column for many years. Her haiku and haibun have appeared in noted journals and anthologies, including *New Resonance 12* (Red Moon Press, 2021). Her chapbook *It Always Comes Back* was a winner of the 2020 Snapshot Press eChapbook Award. She currently serves as coordinator for The Haiku Foundation's Touchstone Award for Haibun. An avid birder and naturalist, she lives on the coast of Maine and visits islands as often as she can.